Sports

by Elizabeth Moore

Consultant:
Adria F. Klein, Ph.D.
California State University, San Bernardino

capstone
classroom
Heinemann Raintree • Red Brick Learning
division of Capstone

Sports are fun.

Every sport has rules.

There are rules about where you play.

There are rules about what you wear.

There are rules about what you play with.

These rules keep you safe.

There are rules about how many players are on a team.

There are rules about playing as a team.

Rules tell players what their jobs are.

Rules tell how a game starts.

Rules tell how to score points.

Rules tell how to keep the score.

Rules tell how long a game lasts.

Rules tell about winning and losing.

Rules tell us to play fair.